AF587367

PEGASUS ENCYCLOPEDIA LIBRARY

# Physics

# MOTION

Edited by: Anil Kumar Tomar, Pallabi B. Tomar
Managing editor: Tapasi De
Designed by: Vijesh Chahal, Anil Kumar and Rohit Kumar
Illustrated by: Suman S. Roy, Tanoy Choudhury
Colouring done by: Vinay Kumar, Sonu, Kiran Kumari & Pradeep Kumar

# CONTENTS

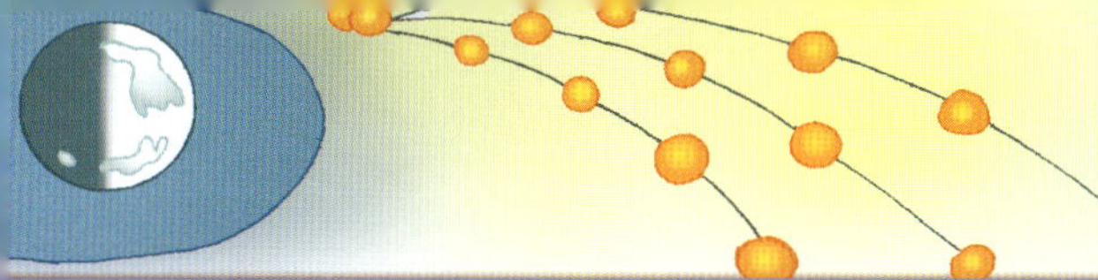



# Introduction

Kinematics is the science of studying the motion of bodies and requires consideration of the geometry and time. It describes the motion of objects using diagrams, numbers, graphs and equations. Kinematics is a branch of mechanics. The goal of kinematics is to develop methods and models which can easily describe and explain the motion of real-world objects; such as movements of airplanes, cars, football kicked by a player, bullet shot by a gun, free falling objects to the surface of Earth, satellites etc.

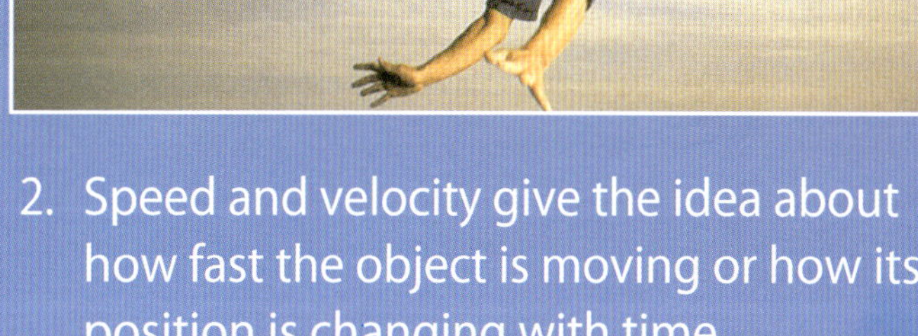

To understand how any object moves, we have to understand three basic elements about what it means when something is moving. These elements describe different parts of exactly how an object moves.

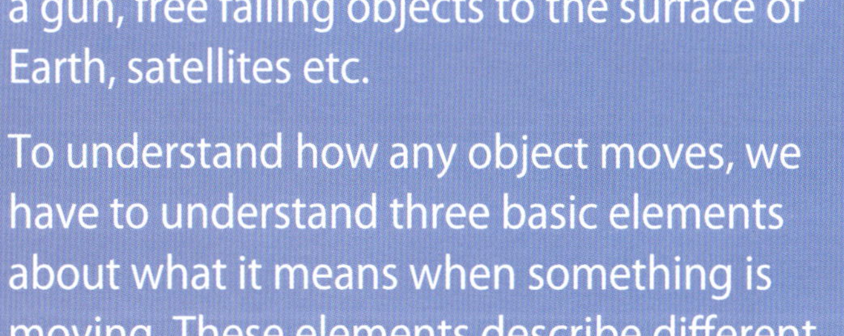

They are:

1. Position and displacement tell exactly where the object was and where is it now.
2. Speed and velocity give the idea about how fast the object is moving or how its position is changing with time.
3. Acceleration tells us about the changes in the object's velocity.

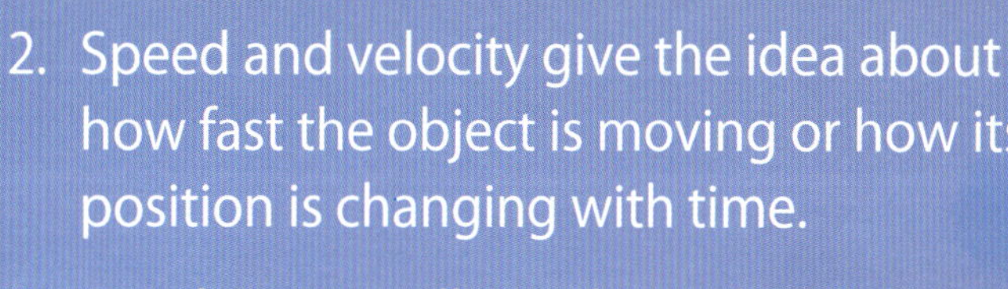

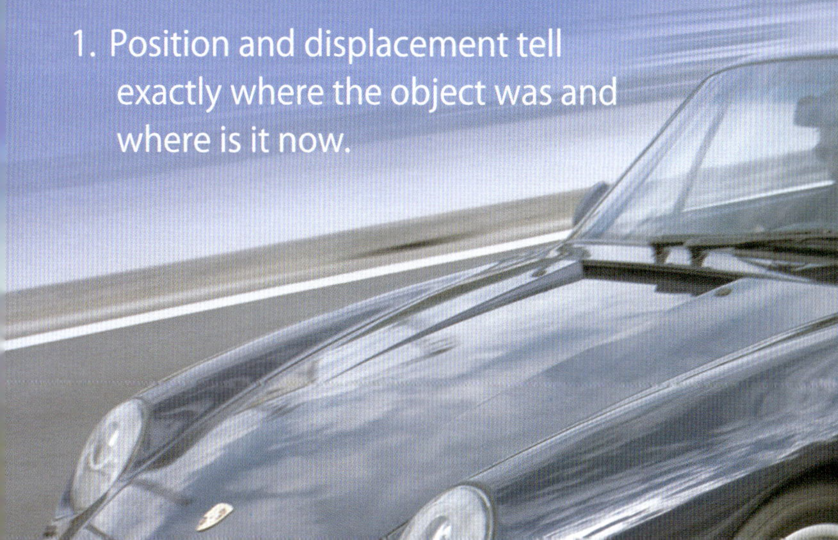

# Scalars and vectors

The motion of objects can be described by elements such as distance, displacement, speed, velocity and acceleration. These mathematical quantities which are used to describe the motion of objects can be divided into two categories—vectors and scalars. These two categories can be distinguished from each other by their distinct definitions.

Scalars are quantities which can be described by magnitude only. For example: time, speed, temperature, distance, mass, volume, density and energy etc. A scalar quantity has no directional component. Suppose an object has a mass of 50kg, then the value of magnitude (50kg) is sufficient to describe mass of this object. We do not need any directional component to further explain the mass. So, mass is a scalar quantity. Similarly, if a vehicle covers a distance of 150 km in two hours, then it has a speed of 75/h. It is independent of direction in which the vehicle moves and also it doesn't matter where it will be after 2vhours. The only information that we need is how much distance it covered. So, speed is also a scalar.

Vectors are quantities which are described by both, magnitude and direction. Direction indicates how the vector is oriented relative to some reference axis. For example, displacement, velocity, force, acceleration etc. If an object is displaced 100 m from its initial position, then only magnitude of displacement is not enough to determine the final position of the object. We need to tell about the direction of the object with reference to its initial position. Therefore, to describe the displacement of an object, we need magnitude as well as direction of the displacement. So, it is a vector quantity.

**Scalar Quantities**
length, area, volume speed
mass, density pressure
temperature energy, entropy
work, power

**Vector Quantities**
displacement, direction velocity
acceleration momentum
force lift, drag, thrust weight

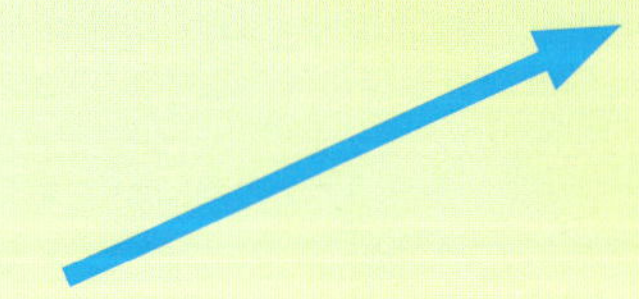

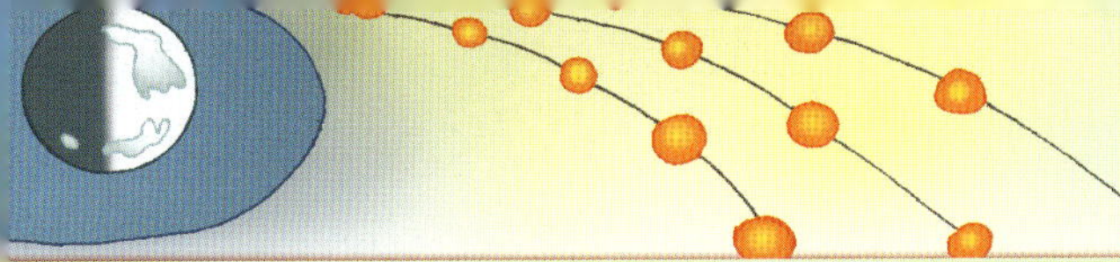



# Reference point, frame of reference and position

To start studying motion of an object, the very first thing that we should know is its initial position. The word 'position' tell us where an object is at a particular time. In science, saying that an object is here or there, is meaningless. We should specify an object's position and direction relative to a known reference point.

A frame of reference is generally defined as a reference point combined with a set of directions. For example, a boy is standing still inside a train when it leaves out of a station. You are standing on the platform and watching the train moving from left to right. It looks as if the boy is moving from left to right, because relative to your position (the platform), he is moving. But according to the boy, and his frame of reference (the train), he is not moving. A frame of reference must have an origin and at least a direction. If someone else had been looking at the same boy from some other place, his frame of reference would have been different.

A position is the measurement of an object's location at a given time with reference to an origin. Positions can therefore be negative or positive. The symbol 'x' is used to indicate position. The units of position are same as units of length; for example, centimetre (cm), metre (m) or kilometre (km).

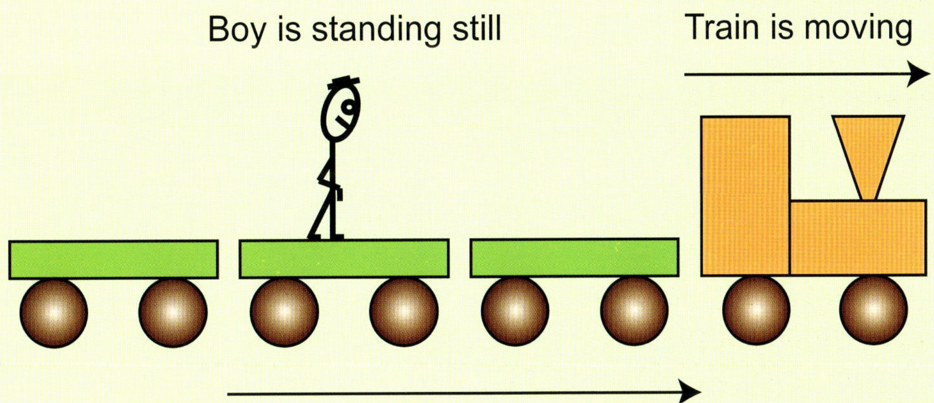

You are standing still on the platform

# Distance and displacement

Distance and displacement are two quantities that may seem to mean the same thing but essentially have distinct meanings.

The displacement of an object is defined as the change in its position. Displacement has a magnitude and direction and is therefore a vector. For example, if the initial position of an object is $x_i$ and it moves to a final position of $x_f$, then the displacement can be calculated as: $x_f - x_i$

Subtraction of an initial quantity from a final quantity in Physics is very common. The delta (Δ) is a Greek letter and is used in Mathematics and Science to indicate a change in a certain quantity, or a final value minus an initial value. For example, $\Delta x$ means change in x while $\Delta t$ means change in t. Therefore, displacement can be written as $\Delta x$. Thus,

$\Delta x = x_f - x_i$

Displacement does not depend on the path travelled, but only on the initial and final positions. Thus, displacement is the shortest distance from the starting point to the endpoint.

The word distance is used to describe how far an object travels along a particular path. Distance is the actual path that was covered by an object. Distance is indicated by symbol d and does not have a direction. So it is a scalar quantity.

## Do it yourself

**Experiment for Newton's third law:** A seated child can kick his legs out to propel himself and his chair backward. This is the same principle as a rocket in space that can accelerate even without an atmosphere to push off (like an airplane requires).

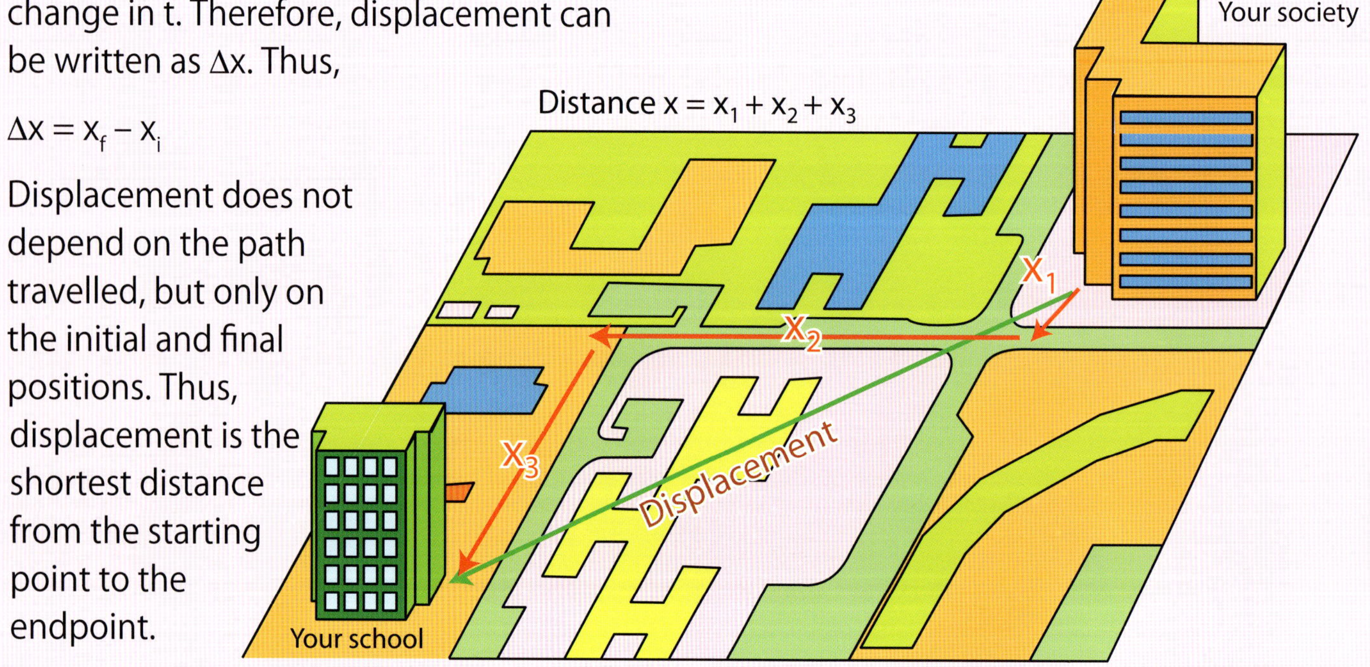

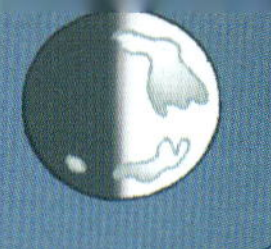

# Velocity

Velocity is defined as the rate of change of position. It is used to determine how the position of a moving object is changing with time. It is represented by symbol 'v'. The velocity can be calculated as the displacement divided by the time taken. If an object has $\Delta x$ displacement in t, velocity (v) is mathematically defined as:

Velocity = displacement / time

$v = \Delta x / t$

Since displacement is a vector, velocity is also a vector. Velocity can be positive or negative. Positive values of velocity tell that the object is moving away from the reference point or origin and negative values mean that the object is moving towards the reference point or origin. The unit of velocity is metre per second [m/s].

## Average velocity

Average velocity is calculated as the total displacement divided by the total time. If an object reaches point B from its initial position A in time $t_1$, from B to C in time $t_2$ and from C to D in time $t_3$. Then its average velocity (vavg) can be given as,

$v_{avg} = d\ (A \rightarrow D) / t_1 + t_2 + t_3$

If the velocity of the object is changing at a uniform rate, then average velocity is given by the arithmetic mean of initial velocity (u) and final velocity (v) for a given period of time. That is,

Average velocity =initial velocity +final velocity / 2

Mathematically, $v_{avg}$ =u +v/2

## Do it yourself

**Experiment for Newton's third law:** Attach equal weights with a string and hang them off opposite sides of a table, with spring scales inserted between mass and string to measure the opposing force each weight experiences. The equality of the readings demonstrates the third law. The equality will hold for unequal weights as well.

# Speed

Speed is defined as the total distance travelled in the unit time. In order to calculate the speed of an object we must know how far it's gone and how long it took to get there. Distance and time are scalars and therefore speed will also be a scalar. It is independent of direction in which the vehicle moves and also it doesn't matter that where it was after a given time. The only information we need is how much distance it covered in a defined time period. We can say that speed is the rate of change of distance with time. Speed can be calculated as distance travelled divided by the time taken,

Speed = distance / time

$s = d / t$

We know that the object moving faster (the one with the greater speed) will go farther than the one moving slower in the same amount of time. Either that or they'll tell you that the one moving faster will get where it's going before the slower one. Whatever the speed is, it always involves both distance and time. If the speed of an object is doubled, it will travel the double distance in a given amount of time. Also, doubling speed of an object would mean halving the time required to travel a given distance.

**Instantaneous speed** is the speed at any instant of time. A car's speedometer shows its instantaneous speed, that is, the speed determined over a very small interval of time — an instant. Ideally, this interval should be as close to zero as possible, but in reality we are limited by the sensitivity of our measuring devices.

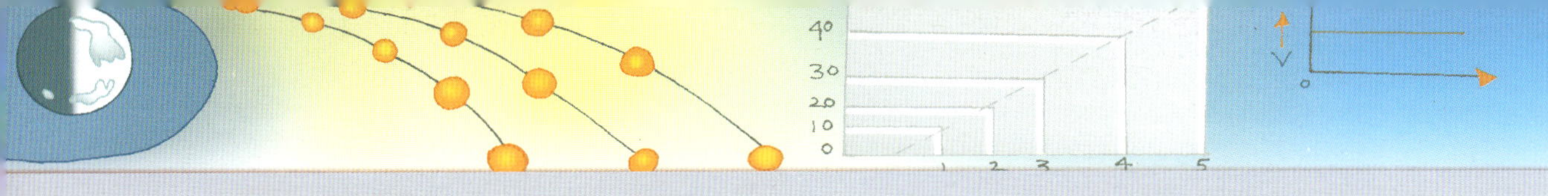

**Example: Harry drives his car 2 km away from home in 30 minutes. He then turns his car around and drives back home along the same path. Again he covers that distance in 30 minutes. Calculate the average speed and average velocity of the car.**

**Solution:** Total distance travelled (d) = 2 + 2 = 4 km

Total time taken to travel the total distance (Δt) = 30 + 30 = 60 minutes

Convert all the distances into SI units:

We know that: 1 km = 1 000 m and 1 min = 60 s

Thus, 4 km = 4 000 m and 60 min = 3600 s

The car started at home and returned home. Thus, by definition, the displacement is 0 m.

$\Delta x = 0$ m

Average speed (s) = d/Δt

=4 000 m/3 600 s

= 1.11 m/s

Average velocity (v) = Δx/Δt

= 0 m/3 600 s

= 0 m/s

ome

Car

30 minute

2 k

ROAD

ome

Car

30 minute

2 k

ROAD

# Acceleration

The rate of change of velocity is called acceleration. Acceleration is the measure of how fast the velocity of an object changes with respect to time. It is represented by symbol 'a'. If $\Delta v$ is the change in velocity over a time interval ($\Delta t$), then the acceleration ($a$) can be calculated as:

Acceleration = change in velocity / change in time

$$a = \Delta v / \Delta t$$

The units of velocity and time are metres per second [m/s] and second [s] respectively. Calculating acceleration involves dividing velocity by time or in terms of units, dividing meters per second [m/s] by second [s]. Thus, the standard unit of acceleration is [m/s2].

Since velocity is a vector, acceleration is also a vector. Acceleration does not provide any information about a motion. The acceleration cannot be used to determine how fast an object is moving or in which direction. It only tells us how the motion of an object changes with time. Acceleration can be negative or positive. If the sign of the acceleration and the velocity are the same, the object is speeding up. If both velocity and acceleration are positive, the object is speeding up in a positive direction. If both velocity and acceleration are negative, the object is speeding up in a negative direction. If velocity is positive and acceleration is negative, then the object is slowing down. Similarly, if the velocity is negative and the acceleration is positive the object is slowing down.

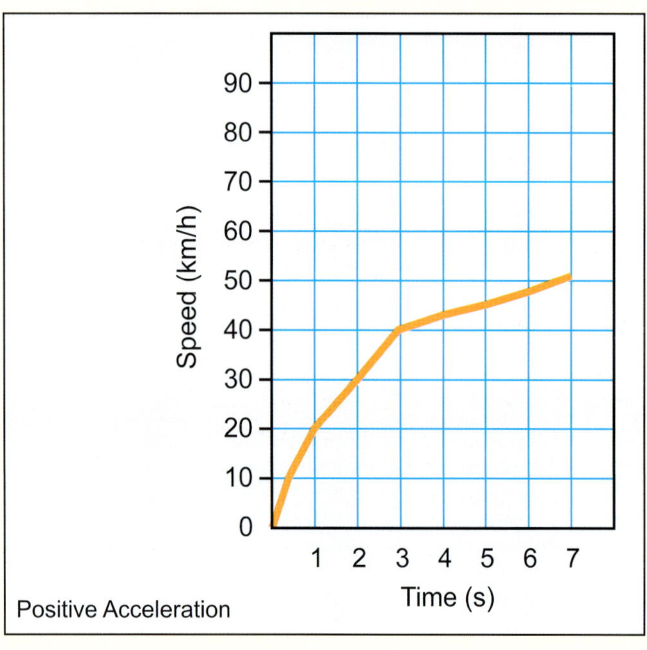

Positive Acceleration

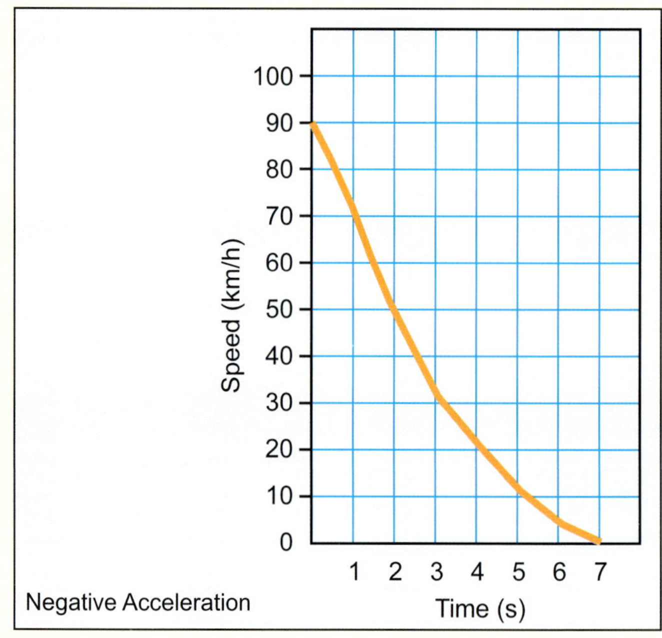

Negative Acceleration

**Example: A car accelerates uniformly with initial velocity of 2 m/s to a final velocity of 10 m/s in 8 seconds. It then slows down uniformly to a final velocity of 4 m/s in 6 seconds. Calculate the acceleration of the car during the first 8 seconds and during the last 6 seconds.**

Solution

For the first 8 seconds:

Initial velocity, $u = 2$ m/s,

Final velocity, $v = 10$ m/s

$\Delta v = 10 - 2 = 8$ m/s

$\Delta t = 8$ s

$a = \Delta v / \Delta t$

$= 8/8$

$= 1$ m/s$^2$

For the last 6 seconds:

$u = 10$ m/s

$v = 4$ m/s

$\Delta v = 4 - 10 = -6$ m/s

$\Delta t = 6$ s

$a = \Delta v / \Delta t$

$= -6/6$

$= -1$ m/s$^2$

# Motion diagrams

Equations are great for describing idealized situations, but they don't always cut it. Sometimes you need a picture to show what's going on; a mathematical picture called a **graph**. Graphs are often the best way to convey descriptions of real world events in a compact form. Graphs of motion come in several types depending on which of the kinematic quantities (time, displacement, velocity, acceleration) are assigned to which axis.

- Importance of graphs in characterizing the motion of the objects:
- Graphs can easily be understood at a glance and tell us about the nature of motion
- Plotting graphs takes less time and is more convenient
- With graphs, the position of any moving object at any intermediate point of time can easily be determined without many calculations
- By simply looking at the motion graphs, motion of two moving objects can be easily compared

Motion line graphs are used to show the relation of quantities like displacement, velocity, acceleration or time, with respect to each other. Generally, the motion graphs are generated by plotting displacement, velocity or acceleration of an object (on y-axis) against time (on x-axis). The most common types of motion graphs are,

- Displacement - time graphs
- Velocity - time graphs

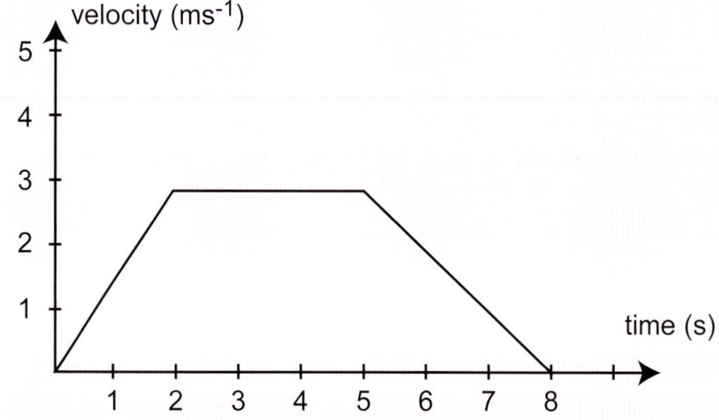


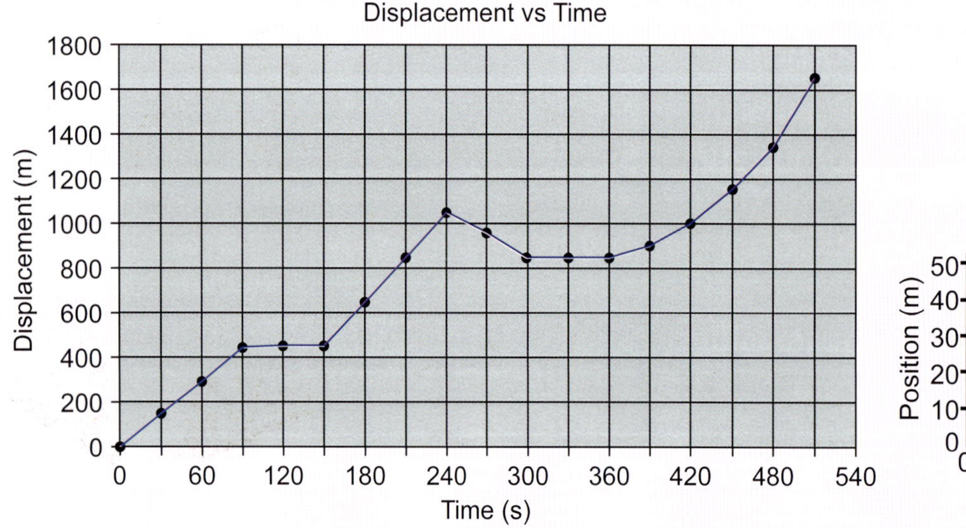


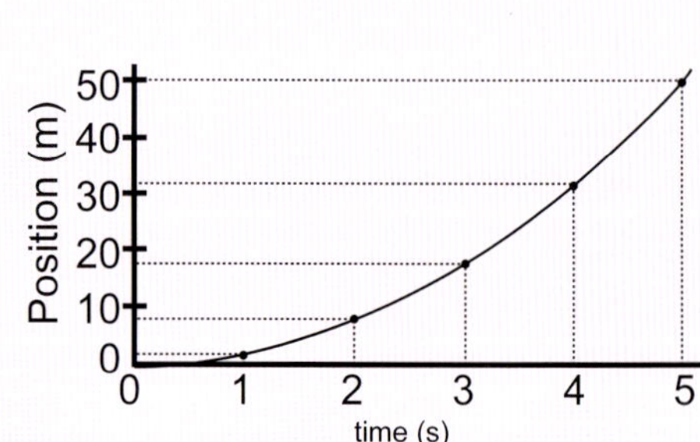

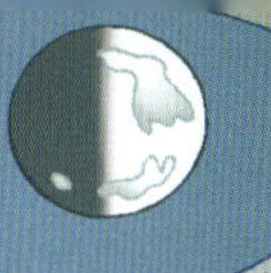

## Displacement-time graphs

The change in the position of an object with respect to time can be represented on the distance-time graphs. In displacement - time graphs, time is taken along the x–axis and distance is taken along the y-axis. We can plot these graphs under various conditions where objects move with uniform speed, non-uniform speed, remain at rest etc.

The displacement - time graphs are generally employed to find the following things about moving objects:

- Nature of the motion of an object
- Position or displacement at any instant of time
- Speed or velocity of a moving object

On a displacement-time graph,

- The slope of line indicates the velocity of the body
- For a stationary body, the displacement time graph is a straight line parallel to the time axis. The slope of the line is zero. The zero slope of line indicates the velocity of the body is zero
- For a body moving with constant velocity, the displacement time graph is a straight line inclined at any angle from the time axis. If the slope is more, the velocity of the body is more and if the slope is less, the velocity of the body is less

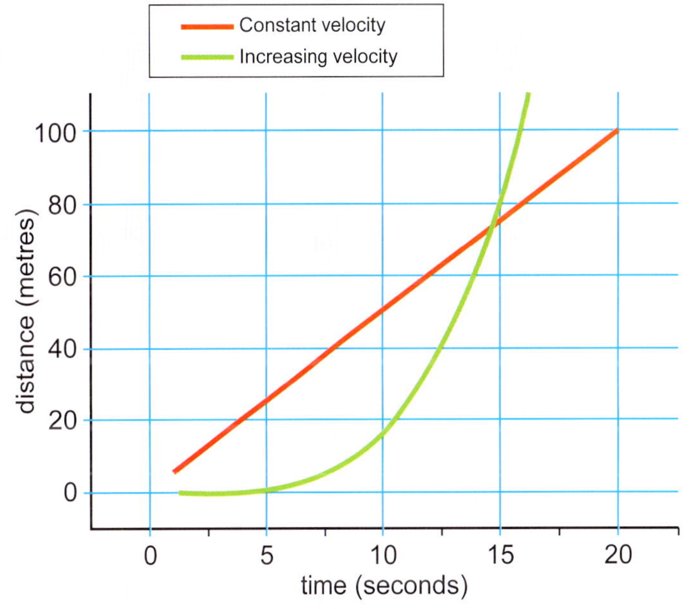


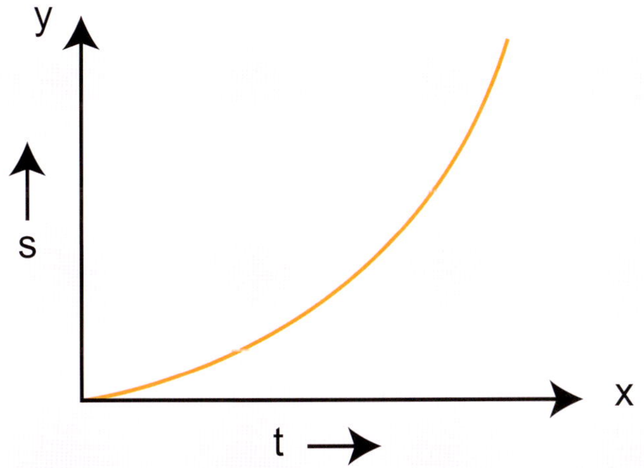


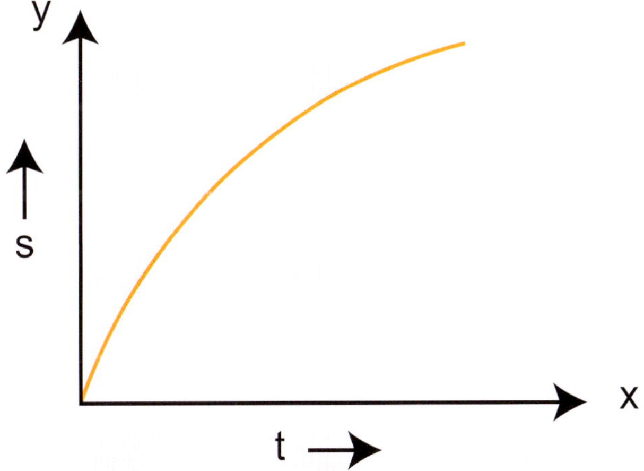

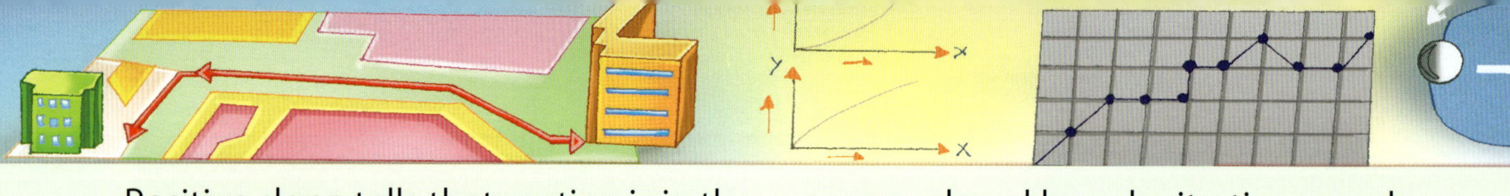

- Positive slope tells that motion is in the positive direction. Similarly, negative slope implies motion in the negative direction
- If we plot motion of two objects and their curves coincide, it means that the two objects have the same displacement at that time

## Velocity-time graphs

The variation in velocity with time for an object can be represented by a velocity-time graph. In these graphs, time is represented along the x-axis and the velocity is represented along the y-axis. If an object moves at uniform velocity, the height of its velocity-time graph will not change with time. It will be a straight line parallel to the x-axis. We know that the product of velocity and time is equal to the displacement of an object moving with uniform velocity. Therefore, area enclosed by velocity-time graph and the time axis is always equal to the displacement.

The following results can be deduced from velocity-time graph:

- The acceleration produced in a body
- The distance covered by a moving object

On a velocity-time graph,

- The slope is equal to acceleration of the object
- Straight line implies that the acceleration is uniform while a curved line indicates non-uniform acceleration
- An object undergoing constant acceleration traces a straight line
- Positive slope implies an increase in velocity in the positive direction and negative slope implies an increase in velocity in the negative direction

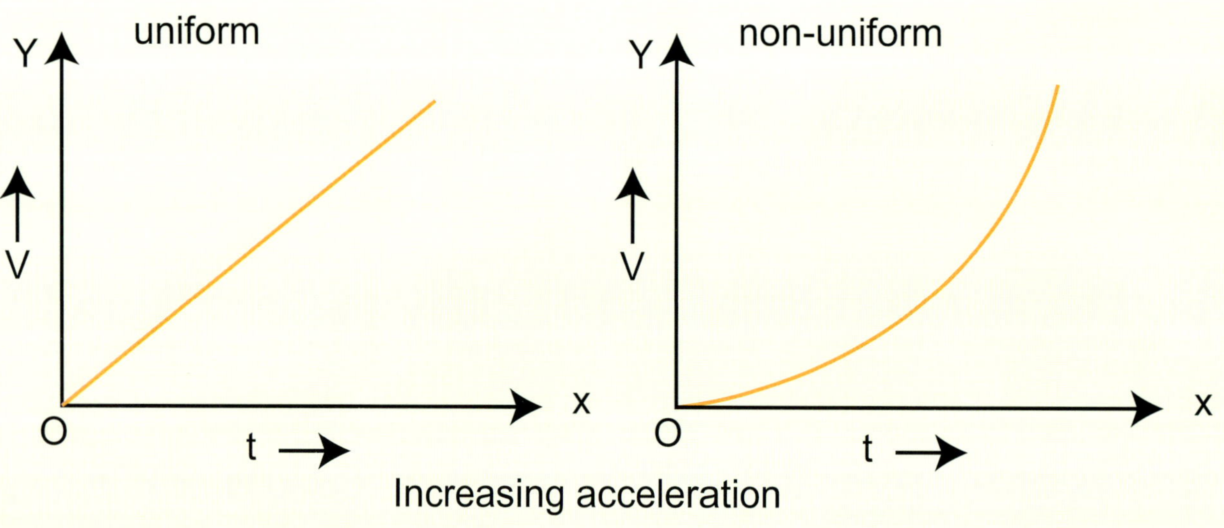

Increasing acceleration

- Zero slope implies motion with constant velocity or no acceleration
- The area under the curve equals the change in displacement
- When two curves coincide, the two objects have the same velocity at that time

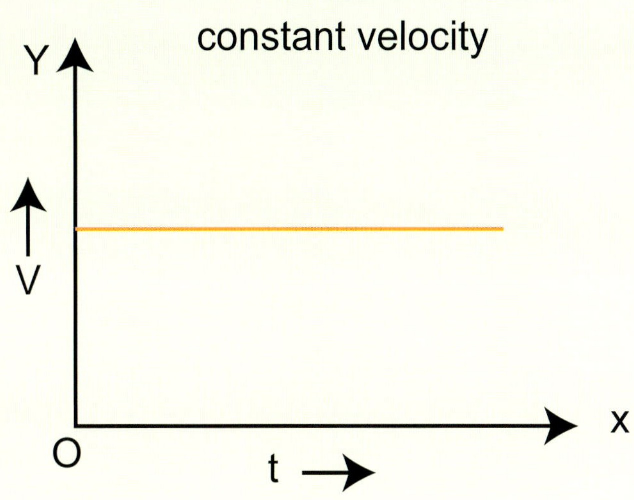


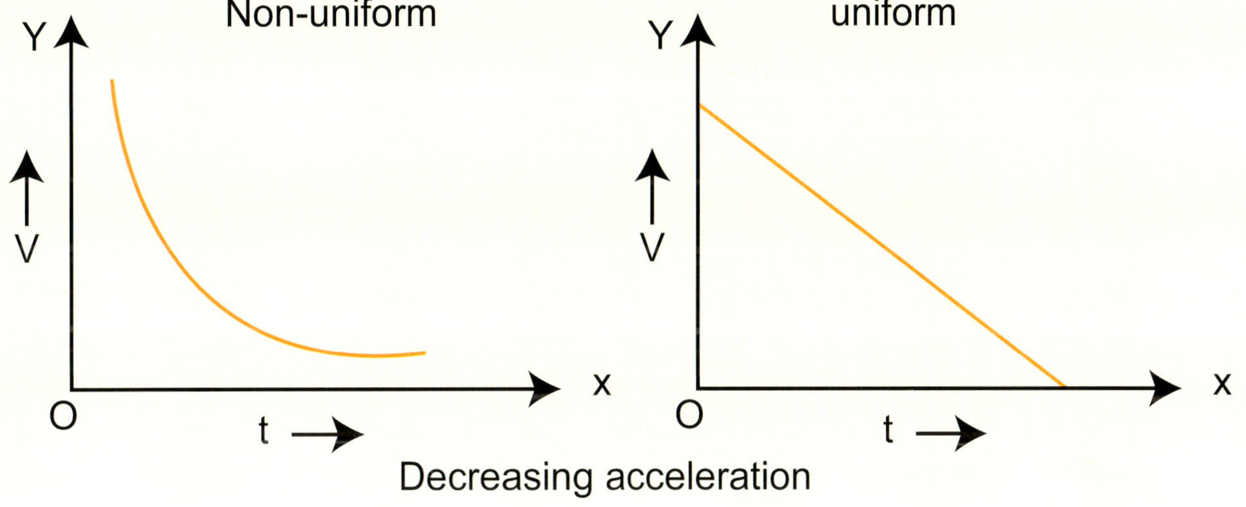


Decreasing acceleration

## Air slows things down

Take two pieces of ordinary paper. Crumple one into a ball. Lift your arms high and drop both pieces of paper at the same time. You will see that the crumpled paper drops right to the ground. The flat sheet floats slowly down.

Explanation: Air resists the movement of objects. The larger the surface pressed on by the air, the harder it is for the object to move through the air. The flat, wing- like sheet of paper has a larger surface than the crumpled paper ball.

# The acceleration due to gravity

When an object falls freely close to the surface of a massive body, it experiences acceleration because of gravity. This is known as the acceleration due to gravity or the acceleration of free fall. Its value can be calculated using the formula

$g = GM / (R + h)^2$

M is the mass of the gravitating body (such as the Earth)

R is the radius of the body, h is the height above the surface

G is the gravitational constant (= 6.6742 × 10–11 $N \cdot m^2 / kg^2$)

If the falling object is very near to the surface of the gravitating body, we can reduce the above equation to

$g = GM / R^2$

In the case of the Earth, the value of g is approximately 9.8 $m/s^2$.

The exact value of g depends on location because of two main factors: the Earth's rotation and the Earth's equatorial bulge.

## Variations in the value of g

The downward force of gravity is opposed by an outward centrifugal force due to the planet's rotation, which is greater at the equator than at higher latitudes. This effect would result in a range of values of g from 9.789 $m/s^2$ at the equator to 9.823 $m/s^2$ at the poles.

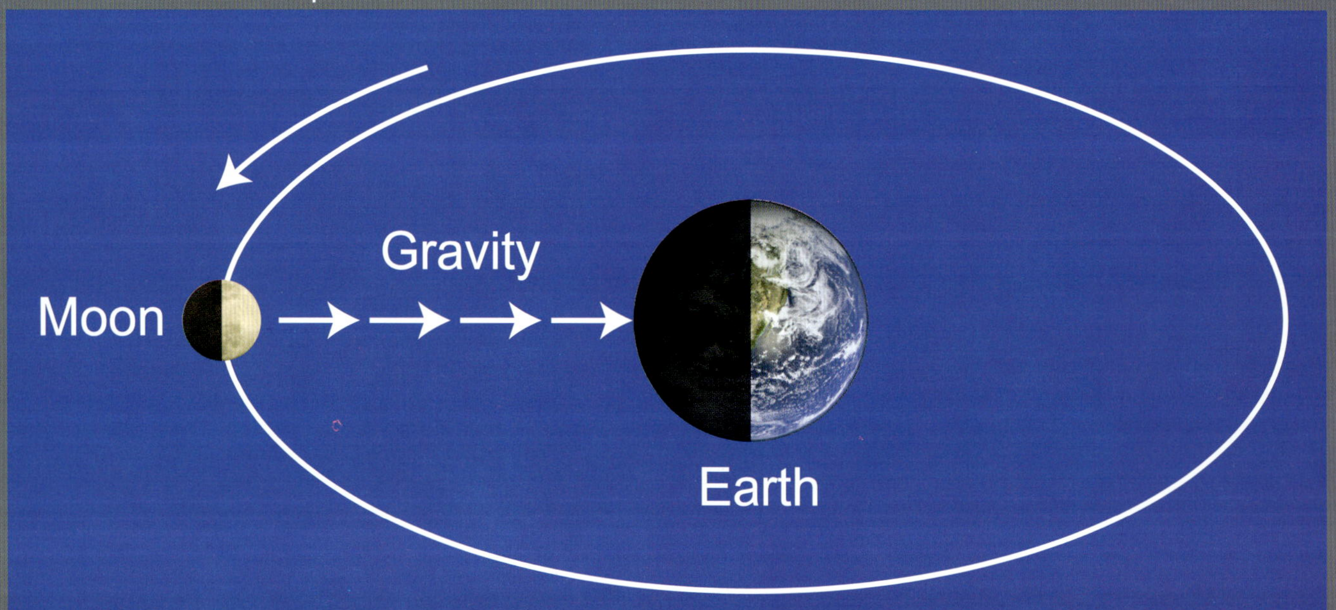

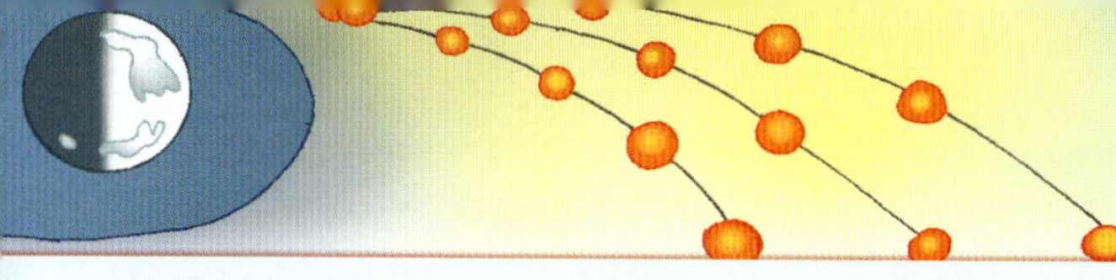



This variation can further be explained by the Earth's equatorial bulge, which causes objects at lower latitudes to be further from the planet's centre than objects nearer the poles and hence subject to a slightly weaker gravitational pull. Physicists have calculated an average value of g over the whole surface of the Earth and derived a standard value for g of 9.8 $m/s^2$. The weight of same objects is varying on different planets and moons due to the different values of the acceleration due to gravity.

Stone

EARTH

## The effect of air resistance

If there were no atmosphere, all free falling objects would fall at the same rate. An object dropped from a very great height would keep accelerating at a rate of 9.8 m/s2 until it hits the ground. But, in practice, this doesn't happen. The reason of this is air resistance. The air resistance is directly proportional to the speed of the falling object. The faster an object falls, more is the air resistance acting on it. At a certain velocity, the downward force of gravity is balanced by the upward force of air resistance and there is no further acceleration. This velocity is known as the terminal velocity.

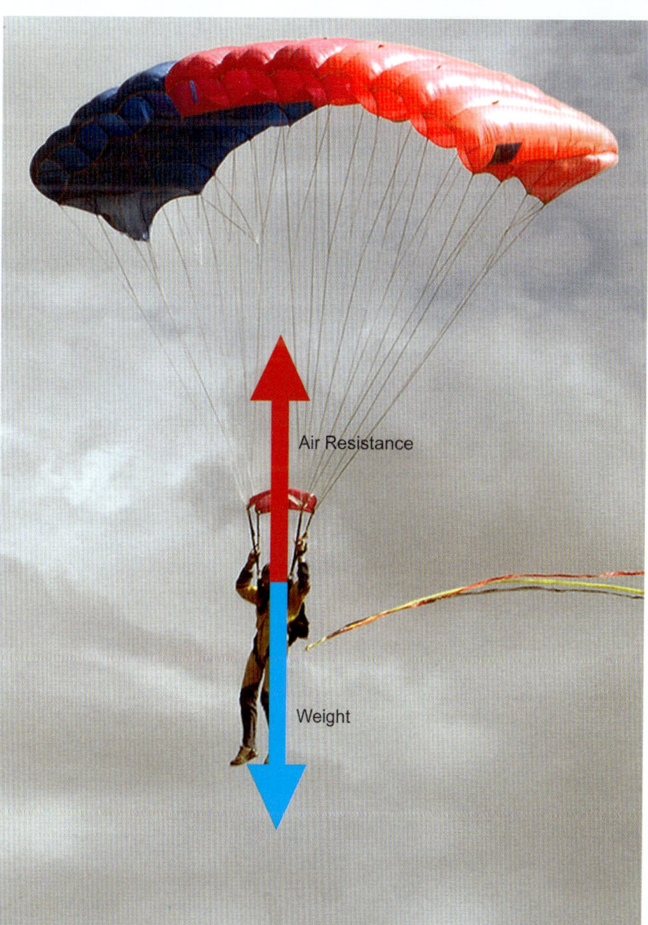

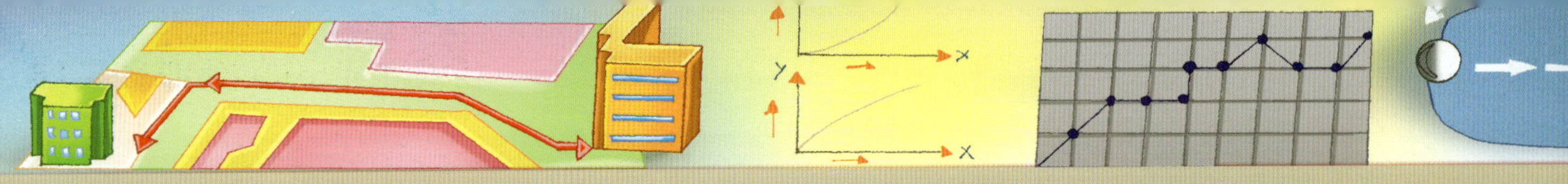

# The motion equations

## Velocity-time

Velocity and time relationship is determined by the first equation of motion. This relationship between velocity and time is very simple if an object is constantly accelerated in a straight-line motion. Constant acceleration always implies a uniform rate of change in the velocity. The higher value of the acceleration tells that there is the greater change in velocity. The change in velocity is directly proportional to time when acceleration is constant. By definition, we know that acceleration can be expressed as

$a = \Delta v / t$

If u is the initial velocity and v is the final velocity of the object, we will have

$a = v - u / t$

$v - u = a \Delta t$

$v = u + a \Delta t$

This is the first and the most simple equation of motion. The last part of this equation at is the change in the velocity from the initial value. We know that 'a' is the rate of change of velocity in time't' since the object had its initial velocity 'u'.

Thus, if an object is accelerating at 10 m/$s^2$, after 5 s it would be moving 50 m/s faster than it was initially. If it started with a velocity of 15 m/s, its velocity after 5 s of acceleration would be 15 + 50 = 65 m/s.

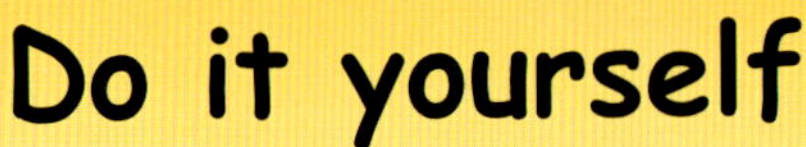


**Experiment for Newton's first Law:** Drop a tennis ball lightly onto carbon paper, marking blank paper underneath. Then hurl the tennis ball at the carbon paper. The latter makes a larger mark because its inertia keeps it in motion.

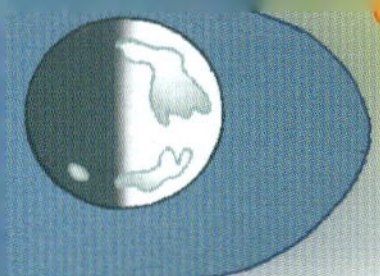



# Displacement-time

We know that displacement of a moving object is directly proportional to both velocity and time. So, an object moving faster always goes farther. Now the velocity is also directly proportional to time. Therefore, it implies that displacement is proportional to the square of the time. For example, a car accelerating for two seconds would cover four times the distance of a car accelerating for only one second ($2^2 = 4$). A car accelerating for three seconds would cover nine times the distance ($3^2 = 9$).

By definition, the velocity can be expressed as

$v = \Delta x / t$

$\Delta x = v\,t$

If an object starts moving from position x0 and stops at x, then

$x - x_0 = v\,t$

As displacement is in part directly proportional to time and in part directly proportional to time squared. We can write it as

$x - x_0 = u\,t + \frac{1}{2} a\,t^2$

If there is no acceleration, then the velocity is constant, which means that the initial velocity is the same as the final velocity. The acceleration term at the end accounts that the velocity is changing. A positive acceleration would increase the displacement and a negative acceleration would decrease it. If velocity of an object increases, it moves farther than if it moves at a constant velocity. Similarly, if an object's velocity decreases, it would have a smaller displacement than if it moves with constant velocity.

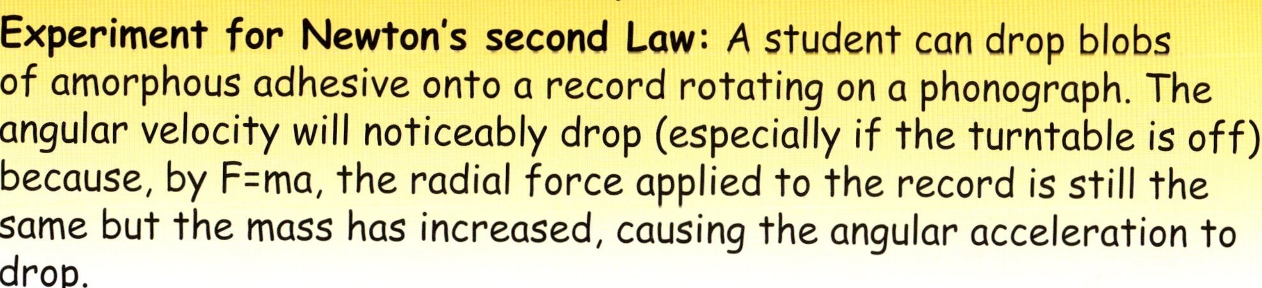

## Do it yourself

**Experiment for Newton's second Law:** A student can drop blobs of amorphous adhesive onto a record rotating on a phonograph. The angular velocity will noticeably drop (especially if the turntable is off) because, by F=ma, the radial force applied to the record is still the same but the mass has increased, causing the angular acceleration to drop.

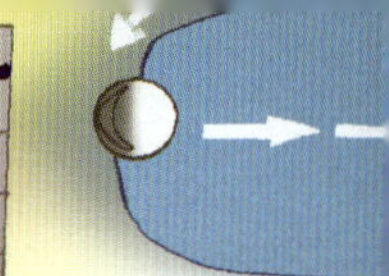

# Velocity-displacement

The first two equations of motion describe kinematic variables velocity and displacement as a function of time. From these equations, we have learnt that

1. Velocity is directly proportional to time when acceleration is constant ($v \propto t$).
2. Displacement is proportional to time squared when acceleration is constant ($s \propto t^2$).

Combination of these two equations, gives rise to a third equation of motion that is independent of time. This equation states that

3. Displacement is proportional to velocity squared when acceleration is constant ($s \propto v^2$).

From the first equation of motion, we know that

$v = u + at$

$v - u = at$ ……(a)

We know that, velocity = $\Delta x / t$

We also know that, average velocity = $u + v / 2$

Thus, $\Delta x / t = u + v / 2$ …… (b)

Multiplying equations (a) and (b), we get

$(v - u)\ (v + u) / 2 = (a\ t)\ (\Delta x / t)$

$(v - u)\ (v + u) = 2\ a\ \Delta x$

$v^2 - u^2 = 2\ a\ \Delta x$

## Do it yourself

**Experiment for Newton's third law:** Newton's Cradle is a set of strung marbles hanging as pendulums in contact. If some of them are raised, and allowed to drop down into the marbles at rest, the same number of marbles will be propelled off the other side. Though the exact behavior is dictated by the conservation of momentum and energy, the equality of incoming and outgoing marbles also demonstrates the third law.

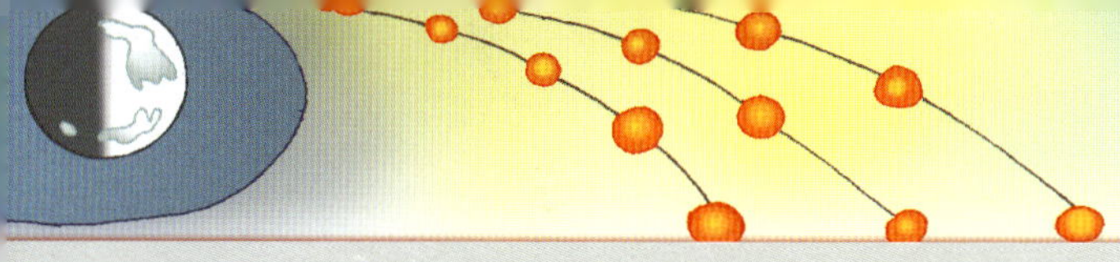



# Momentum

Momentum is defined as 'mass in motion'. All objects have mass. So, all moving objects have momentum. The amount of momentum that an object has is dependent upon two variables— the mass of moving object and velocity. In terms of an equation, the momentum of an object is equal to the mass of the object times the velocity of the object. In physics, momentum is represented by symbol 'p'.

Momentum = mass . velocity

$p = m \cdot v$

Where, m is the mass and v is the velocity of the moving object. The equation illustrates that momentum is directly proportional to an object's mass and directly proportional to the object's velocity. From the definition of momentum, it becomes obvious that an object has a large momentum if either its mass or its velocity is large. Both variables are of equal importance in determining the momentum of an object. The momentum of any object that is at rest is 0. Objects at rest do not have momentum; they do not have any 'mass in motion'. Both variables - mass and velocity - are important in comparing the momentum of two objects. The standard unit of momentum is the kg•m/s. Momentum is a vector quantity. To fully describe the momentum of a 10 kg object moving westward at 5 m/s, we must include information about both the magnitude and the direction of the object. It is not enough to say that the momentum of the object is 50 kg•m/s. The momentum of the object is not fully described until information about its direction is given. The direction of the momentum vector is the same as the direction of the velocity. The direction of the velocity vector is the same as the direction that an object is moving. If the object is moving westward, then its momentum can be fully described by saying that it is 50 kg•m/s, westward.

At 25, Physicist Lawrence Bragg is the youngest person to receive a Nobel Prize.

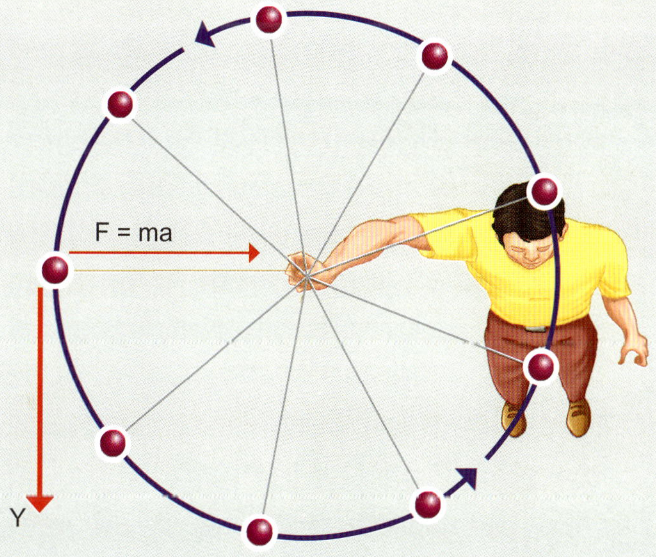

# Newton's laws of motion

Three laws of motion were deduced by Sir Isaac Newton (1642-1727) to describe the motion of objects under influence of force.

## First Law of Motion

Newton suggested that a stationary object remains stationary until and unless a force acts on it. Similarly, a moving object will continue moving unless a force slows it down, speeds it up or changes its direction of motion. This is known as Newton's first law of motion and states that

**"An object will remain in a state of rest or continue moving with a constant velocity, until or unless acted upon by an external force."**

And so we see that this law deals with forces and changes in velocity. We experience this law in everyday life. For example, the force of the exploding gases pushes the rocket through the air into space. Once it is in space, the engines are switched off and it will keep on moving at a constant velocity. If the astronauts want to change the direction of the spaceship they need to fire an engine. This will then apply a force on the rocket and it will change its direction. Similarly, seat belts, that protect us when the car is involved in an accident, are based on this principle. If a car is travelling at high speed and the car suddenly stops, a force is exerted on the car (making it slow down), but not on the passengers. The passengers will carry on moving forward at high speed according to first law of motion. If they are wearing seat belts, the seat belts will stop them by exerting a force on them and so prevent them from getting hurt.

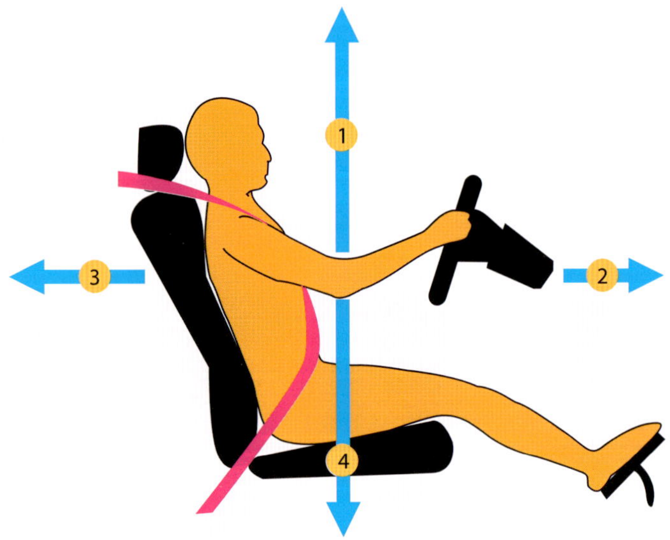

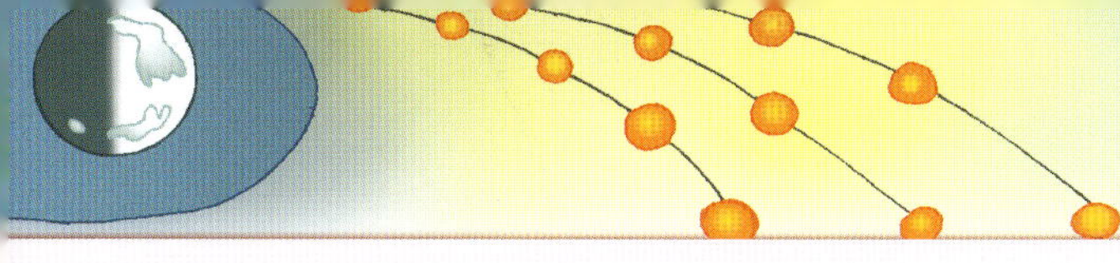



## Second law of motion

Newton's second law of motion explains how an object will change velocity if it is pushed or pulled upon. This is also known as the law of force. According to this law, if a resultant force acts on an object, it accelerates, that is, it changes its velocity in the direction of the force. Secondly, this acceleration is directly proportional to the force. For example, if we push an object to accelerate it, the acceleration will be greater for a hard push and lower for a soft push. Also, this acceleration is inversely proportional to the mass of the object. For example, if we push two objects equally, the object having lesser mass will accelerate more and the one having more mass will have less acceleration.

Newton's second law of motion states that,

**"The rate of change of linear momentum of a body is directly proportional to the external unbalanced force acting on it".**

Mathematically,

$F = ma$

Applications of second law of motion

1. Man pulling a box
2. Truck and trailer
3. Lifts

## Third law of motion

Newton's third law of motion explains the interaction between pairs of objects. If body A exerts a force $F_1$ on body B, then body B exerts a force $F_2$ on body A which is of equal magnitude as $F_1$ and acts in the opposite direction. Thus,

$$F_1 = -F_2$$

This law states that

**"For every action (force) in nature there is an equal and opposite reaction."**

Newton's action-reaction pairs can be found everywhere in life where two objects interact with one another. For an aircraft, the principle of action and reaction is very important. It can explain the generation of lift from an airfoil. The air is deflected downward by the action of the airfoil, and in reaction the wing is pushed upward with the same force. Similarly, a jet engine also produces thrust through action and reaction. The engine produces hot exhaust gases that flow out the back of the engine. As a reaction, a thrusting force is produced in the opposite direction.

In 2003, archaeologists from Bond University discovered some fossils of human footprints in the Australian Outback. They date back 20,000 years and an analysis of the gait has shown that one of the males (known as T8) was running at 23 mph.

Rocket Engine Thrust

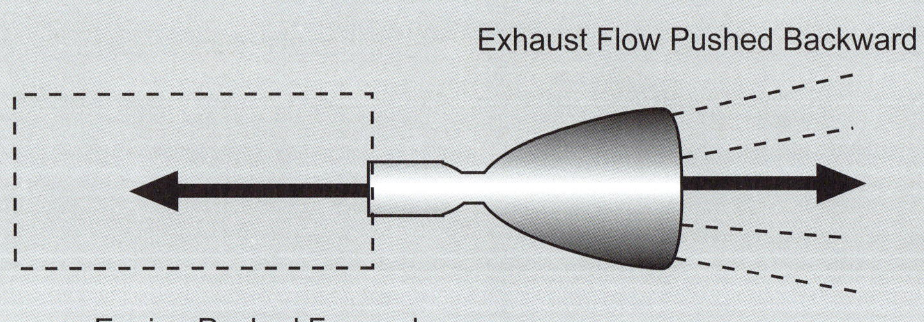

# Impulse

Impulse is defined as the product of the net force and the time interval for which the force acts. Mathematically, impulse is calculated as:

Impulse $= F \cdot \Delta t$

We cal also define impulse as the change in momentum of an object.

Impulse $= mv - mv_0$

$F\Delta t = m\Delta v$

$= \Delta p$

So, for a given change in momentum, $F\Delta t$ is fixed. Thus, if force is reduced, $\Delta t$ must be increased for achieving same change in momentum (that is, a smaller force must be applied for longer time to bring about the same change in momentum).

Alternatively if $\Delta t$ is reduced (that is, the force is applied for a shorter period) then the force must be increased to bring about the same change in momentum.

The important applications of impulse are in improving safety measures and reducing injuries. In many emergency cases like road accidents or sport events, an object needs to be brought to rest from a certain initial velocity. This means there is a certain specified change in momentum. If the time of momentum changes can be increased then the intensity of the force acting will be less and it will cause less damage. This is the main principle of arrestor beds for trucks, airbags in vehicles etc.

# Conservation of momentum

Dealing with momentum is difficult than mass and energy because momentum is a vector quantity; that is, it has both, a magnitude and a direction. It is even more difficult in case of a gas because forces in one direction can affect the momentum in another direction because of the collisions of many molecules.

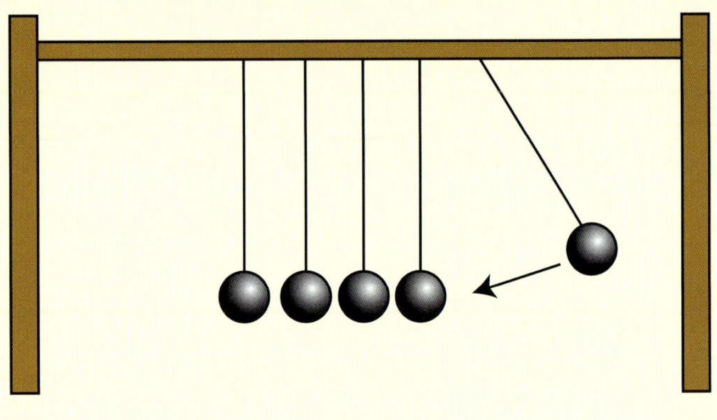

We know that the momentum of a moving object is the product of its mass and velocity. Like the conservation of energy and the conservation of mass, conservation of momentum is also a fundamental concept of physics. This law states that,

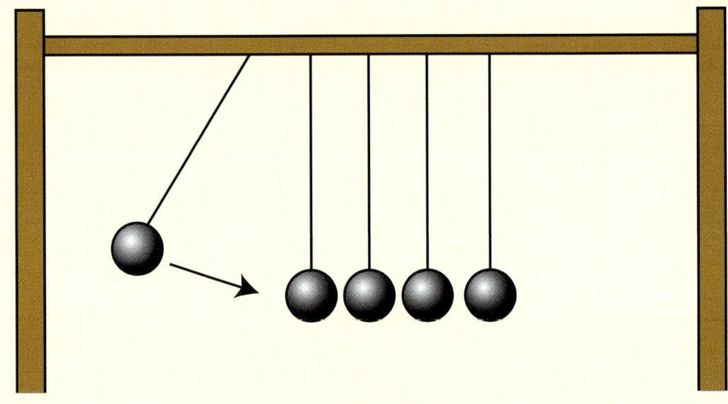

**"The amount of momentum of a closed system remains constant. It can neither be created nor destroyed."**

Consider a collision occurring between two objects in an isolated system. According to the law of conservation of momentum, the total momentum of the two objects before the collision is equal to the total momentum of the two objects after the collision. Therefore, the momentum lost by one object is equal to the momentum gained by second object. In simple way it can be said that the total momentum of a collection of objects is conserved or the total amount of momentum is a constant or unchanging value.

Now let us apply Newton's third law to this collision. In such a collision, the forces acting between the two objects will be equal in magnitude and opposite in direction. Mathematically, this statement can be expressed as

$$F_1 = -F_2$$

These forces act between the two objects for a given amount of time. Sometimes, this time is long and sometimes, it is short. Regardless of how long the time is, the time that the force acts upon one object is always equal to the time that the force acts upon second object. This can be stated as

$$t_1 = t_2$$

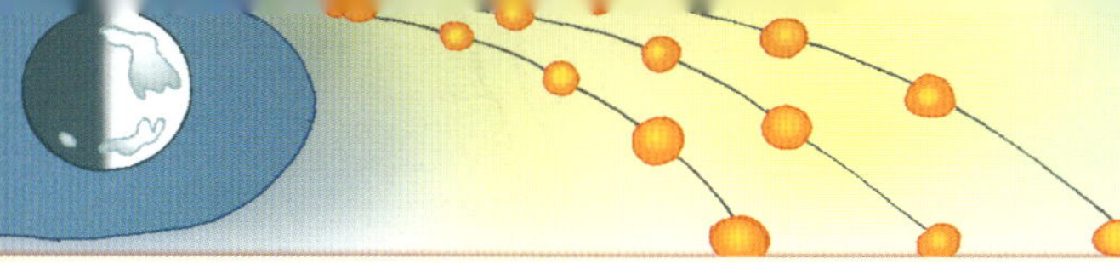



Since, the forces between the two objects are equal and they act for same time, we can say

$F_1 * t_1 = -F_2 * t_2$

So, we can say that the impulses experienced by the two objects are also equal in magnitude and opposite in direction.

By definition, the impulse experienced by an object is equal to the change in momentum of that object. Thus, it follows logically that they must also experience equal and opposite momentum changes. Thus, it can be expressed as

$m_1 * \Delta v_1 = -m_2 * \Delta v_2$

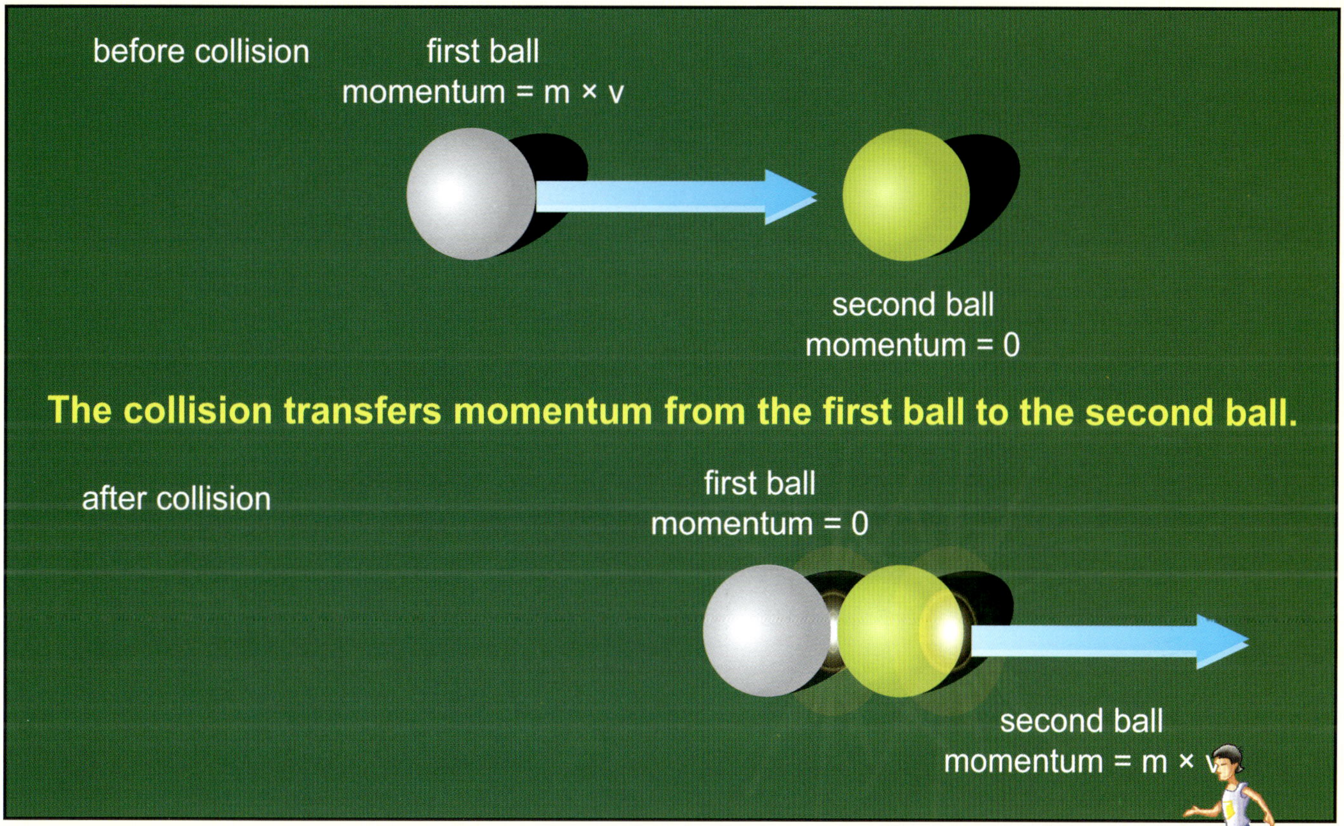

## Do it yourself

**Water pressure:** Punch 3 or 4 small holes, one above the other, along the side of an empty milk carton or a large can. Cover the holes with a long strip of adhesive tape and fill the carton with water. Then place the can in the sink or a basin and pull off the tape. You will see that the stream from the lowest hole travels farthest.

**Explanation:** The water at the bottom of the carton has the force exerted by the pressure of the water above it.

# Projectile motion

A projectile is a free falling object upon which the only force acting is gravity. There are a variety of examples of projectiles. An object dropped from rest is a projectile if the influence of air resistance is negligible. An object that is thrown vertically upward or thrown upward at an angle to the horizontal is also a projectile. Thus, we can define a projectile as any object that once projected or dropped continues in motion by its own inertia and is only influenced by the downward force of gravity.

A projectile motion involves two components of motion – vertical and horizontal. Characteristically, motion in one direction is independent of motion in another direction. Projectile motion is a special case of two dimensional motions with constant acceleration. The basic reason is that force and initial velocity of the object are not along the same direction. The linear motion of the projected object is continuously worked upon by the gravity, which results in the change of both magnitude and direction of the velocity. A change in direction of the velocity ensures that motion is not one dimensional.

Flights of base ball, golf ball, stone thrown from a hill or an object dropped from a building etc. are examples of projectile motion. In these cases, the projectile is projected with certain force at certain angle to vertical or horizontal direction. The force that initiates motion is a contact force.

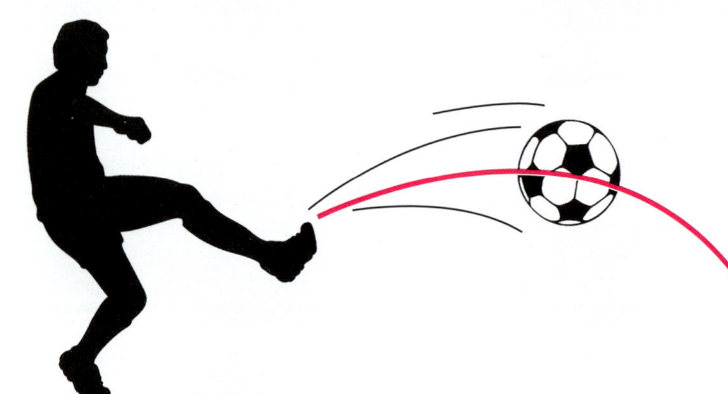

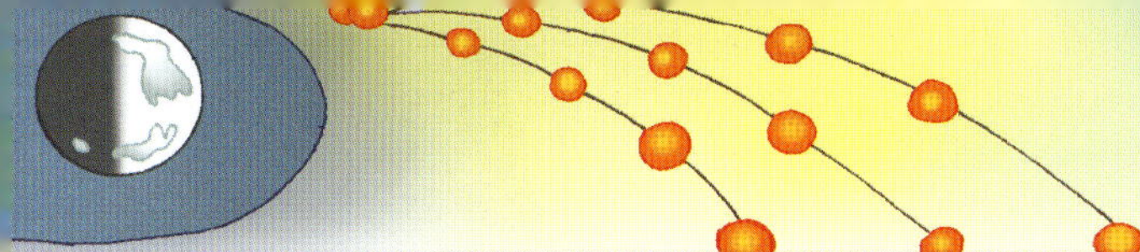



# Essential facts of projectile motion

In order to understand projectile motion, we have to describe three basic facts about it.

1. We know that we need to apply a force at the time of projection to start the motion. This force is either applied by hand or by any other mechanical device. This force accelerates projectile till it is in contact. The moment the projectile is physically disconnected from the throwing device, it moves with a velocity, which it gained during the small contact period.

2. Motion of projectile object is maintained that is, it moves with constant speed if there is no net external force, according to the third law of motion. This would be the case for projection in force free space. Suppose that a projectile motion is initiated into the force free space with an initial velocity, u. The object will continue its motion with constant speed i.e. initial velocity (u).

3. The projectile, in the space, is acted upon by the force due to gravity as well as air resistance. We neglect the effect of air resistance and only consider the motion which is affected only by force due to gravity acting downwards. The motion or velocity of projectile is accelerated by gravity. Thus, acceleration due to gravity (expressed by 'g') is the only acceleration involved in the motion. This downward acceleration is always constant in any projectile motion near earth, which is not propelled or dragged.

Despite its apparent imperial motion, the Earth is pretty speedy. If you stand on the Equator, the speed of its rotation around its own axis is about 1,040mph. This decreases as you approach towards the poles, stand on any pole and you barely move at all.

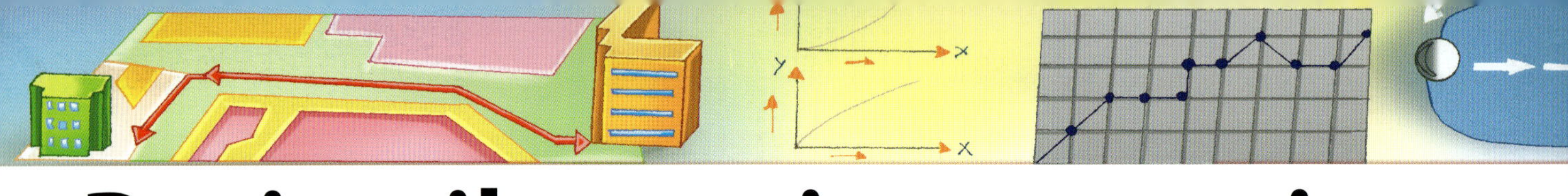

# Projectile motion equations

In vertical direction: Motion of a projectile in vertical direction is moderated by a constant force due to gravity. Therefore, it is described by one dimensional equations of motion for constant acceleration. Suppose an object, in projectile motion, had initial velocity u and accelerating due to gravity with a constant value g.

The velocity (v) in the vertical direction at time t is calculated by

$v = u - gt$

The displacement is given by

$d = ut - \frac{1}{2} gt_2$

The time of flight is given by

$T = 2\ u/g$

**In horizontal direction:** The force of gravity has no component in the horizontal direction. We know that gravitational force is the only force that acts on the projectile. Thus, the motion in horizontal direction is not accelerated if all other components are ignored. By this, we can depict that the motion in horizontal direction is a uniform motion and the component of velocity in x-direction is constant.

The position at horizontal space at a given time t can be calculated by

$X = u * t$

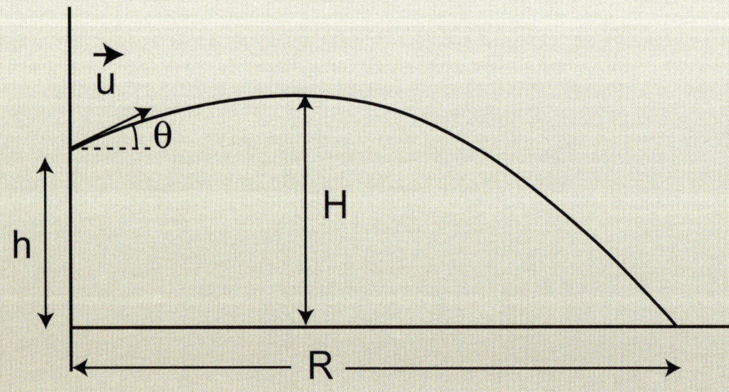


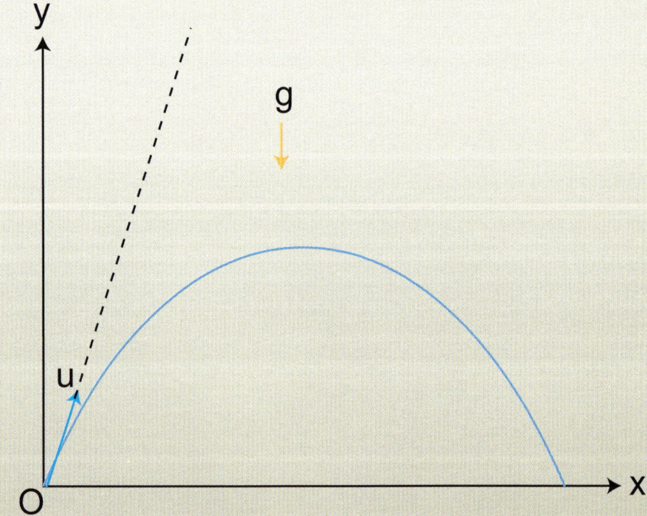

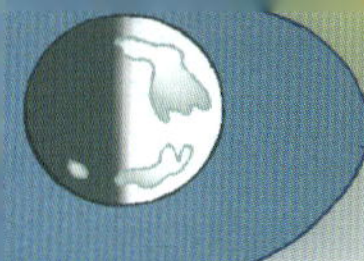

# Test Your MEMORY

1. Define Kinematics.
2. What is the difference between scalar and vector quantities? Give examples.
3. How do we determine speed of a moving object?
4. What is the difference between distance and displacement?
5. What do you understand by conservation of momentum?
6. What is average velocity?
7. Describe Newton's laws of motion.
8. Define impulse?
9. What is acceleration due to gravity?
10. Explain the equation of motion which is independent of time.
11. What do you understand by projectile motion?
12. Write the equations of projectile motion in vertical direction.

# Index